all aboard! John Denver

Piano/Vocal Arrangements by John Nicholas
Cover Photography by Peter Nash

Visit our website at www.cherrylane.com

SALEM PUBLIC LIBRARY

Contents

Peter Nash

There is something in the heart of every human being that responds to a vision of possibility. A better life, true love, fame and fortune, all await us on the far side of the hill. Whether it is a ship under full sail heading out beyond the distant horizon or a spacecraft lifting off toward some bright and shining star, we can't help imagining, if only for a moment, that we might be on board, leaving the past and all of its pain and suffering behind and giving ourselves to the promise of tomorrow. In the light of that promise, any hardship can be endured, devastating loneliness can be tolerated and dreams can and will come true. For me, all of that was personified in the sight and sound of a slow moving freight train heading west.

This album of 14 songs could easily have been twice or three times that number. In researching train songs, I found not only a part of the history of our great country, but a history of music in our country as well. From chain gang hollers to the lonesome sound of the singing brakeman, Jimmie Rodgers. From the free-spirited swing of jazz to the high-spirited kick of bluegrass, and from the simple joy of childhood wonder to the aching sense of loss that comes when a part of who and what we are begins to disappear, perhaps forever.

It is my sincere hope that these few songs will reconnect you to that part of our past and bring some light to the possibility of it being a greater part of our future.

All Aboard !

(Reprinted from the Sony Wonder *Recording)*

Jenny Dreamed Of Trains

Words and Music by
Guy Clark and Vince Gill

When Jen-ny was a lit-tle girl, she on-ly dreamed of trains.___ She nev-er played with dolls___ or lac-y kinds of things.___ Jen-ny count-ed box-

cars_____ in-stead of count-ing sheep_____ 'cause

she could go_____ an-y-where when she went to sleep._

And all she ev-er talked_
The de-pot's_ been board-
Jen-ny laid a pen-

ter school,_____ she'd head down to the track,_____
her when_____ she said she heard the train,_____
ing,_____ all she could find_____

_____ wait - ing for the train_____ that was
said she was just a lit - tle girl
was a lit - tle piece of cop - per squashed_____

nev - er com - ing_____ back.
act - ing kind of_____ strange.
flat - ter than a_____ dime.

Jen - ny

10

dreamed____ of trains.____

Freight Train Boogie/Choo Choo Ch'Boogie (Medley)

Freight Train Boogie
Words and Music by
Kevin Griffin

Choo Choo Ch' Boogie
Words and Music by Vaughn Horton,
Denver Darling and Milton Gabler

on - ly thing ___ that he could un - der - stand ___ was an

G13

Tacet

eight - wheel driv - er un - der his com - mand. ___ He made the

C9

freight train boog - ie all the time. ___

G6

D7

He made the freight train boog - ie as ___

he rode down the line.

Whoo whoo, wah— wah. Whoo whoo, wah—

wah. Whoo whoo, wah— wah.

Whoo whoo, wah— wah. He made the

freight train boog - ie as___ he rolled down the line.___

CHOO CHOO CH'BOOGIE

head - ed for the sta - tion with my pack on my back.__ I'm
reach your des - ti - na - tion and, a - las and a - lack,__ you

3. *Instrumental...*

tired of trans - por - ta - tion in the back of a hack.__ I__
need some com - pen - sa - tion to get back in the black.__ You

just love the rhy - thm of the click - e - ty clack.__ I
take the morn - ing pa - per from the top of the stack__ and

hear the whis - tle blow - ing, see the smoke from the stack. And
read the sit - u - a - tion from the front to the back. The

choo ch'-boog - ie. Take me right back to the track,

Jack. You Take me right back to the

track, Jack. Wa

ba doo ba wa ba doo wa wa ba doo day,_____ wa_____

ba doo ba wa ba doo wa wa ba doo day._____ He made the

freight train boog - ie as_____ he rolled down_____ the line._____

rit.

19

Waiting For A Train

Words and Music by
Jimmie Rodgers

sleep - ing in the rain.___ I walked up to___ a break-
moon and stars___ up a - bove.___ No - bod - y seems___ to want

man just to give him a line___ of talk.___ He
___ me nor to lend me a help - ing hand.___ I'm

said, "If you've - got mon - ey, I'll see that you___ don't walk."_
on my way___ from Fris - co, go - ing back to Dix - ie - land.___

"Well, I have - n't got a nick - el; not a
My pock - et - book is emp - ty; my

Steel Rails

Words and Music by
Louisa Branscomb

rails, chas-ing sun-shine 'round the bend,— wind-ing through the trees—— like a rib-bon in the wind.—— I don't mind not know-ing what lies down the track,—

'cause I'm look-ing out a-head__ to keep__ my

mind from turn-ing__ back.

{ It's not the first__
  The sun is shin -

__ time
ing

I find my-self a-lone at dawn.__
through the o-pen box-car door,__

____ If I real-ly had you once,__ then I__ still
____ ly-ing in my mind__ with__ the

have you when I'm gone._____ Whis - tle
things I've known be - fore._____ And I've lost

blow - ing,_____ blow - ing lone - some in___ my
count of all the hours___ and days___ and

mind,_____ call - ing me a - long___ that nev - er -
time._____ Just the rhy - thm of the rails___ keeps the

end - ing dou - ble_____ line. Steel_____

I've Been Working On The Railroad

Traditional
Arranged by John Denver

way.   Can't   you hear the whis - tle blow   -   ing?

Rise   up so ear - ly in the morn.   Can't   you hear the whis - tle

Faster

blow   -   ing?   Di - nah, blow your horn.   Di -

nah, won't you blow,   Di - nah, won't you blow,

Di - nah, won't you blow your horn?_____ Di - nah, won't you blow, Di -

nah, won't you blow, Di - nah, won't you blow your

Faster

horn? Some - one's in the kitch - en with Di - nah.

Some - one's in the kitch - en, I know._____

30

Some-one's in the kitch-en with Di - nah, strum-ming on the old ban -

Faster

jo. Fee fie fid-dle ee i o, fee___

___ fie fid-dle ee i o._____ Fee fie

Slowly

fid-dle ee i o, strum-ming on the old ban - jo.

On The Atchison, Topeka And The Santa Fe

Music by Harry Warren
Lyric by Johnny Mercer

Whoo___ whoo___ whoo___ whoo.___ She's

got a list of pas - sen - gers that's___ pret - ty big.___ And they'll

all want a lift to Brown's___ Ho - tel___ 'cause

lots of them been trav - el - ing for quite a spell___ all the

35

whiz - zing by.____ Fare thee well Lar - a - mie and Rock - y____

Moun - tain high.____ Yes sir - ree, here we are, go - ing

all the way.__ Must - n't quit till we hit Cal - i - for - ni - a._____

See the old smoke ris - ing

Old Train

Words and Music by
Nikki Pedersen and Herb Pedersen

Old train,_____ I can hear your whis-tle
train,_____ I grow wea-ry at the

blow, and I want_____ to be jump-ing on a - gain._____
miles and I miss_____ the free-dom that was mine._____

Old train,_____ I've been ev - 'ry-where_ you
Old train,_____ just to think_ a-bout_ those

go, and I know what lies be-yond_ each bend. }
times; I'll smile when you're high-ball-ing by. }

Old train, each time you pass,— you're old- er than— the last..

— And it seems— I'm too old for run - ning.——

I hear your rust - y wheels grate a - gainst— the rails;—

— they cry with ev - 'ry mile.——

And I think I'll stay a - while.

Old

Daddy, What's A Train?

Words and Music by
Bruce "U. Utah" Phillips

Dad - dy, what's a train?___ Is it some - thing I___ can ride?___ Does it car - ry lots___ of grown- up folks and lit - tle kids___ in - side?___ Is it

big-ger than our house? Well, how can I____ ex-plain____

____ when my lit-tle boy____ and girl ask____ me,

To Coda ⊕

"Dad-dy, what's a train?"

{ When
  I
  We

clear,   we had to cov - er up our ___ ears,   and we
T - P,   Lack - a - wan - na, ___ the   I   C,   the
did   when I was just a ___ kid,   how

count - ed cars ___ just as high   as we can go.
Nick - el - Plate, ___ the good old San - ta Fe.
far a - way ___ those mem - o - ries ap - pear.

I can al - most hear the steam, ___ those
Just names ___ out of the past, ___ I
I guess ___ it's plain to see ___ they still

The Little Engine That Could

Words by Warren Foster
Music by Billy May

Moderately, in 2

1. There was a lit-tle rail-road train with

2.-5. *See additional lyrics*

loads and loads of toys, all start-ing out to find

choo, choo, choo.— I feel so good to - day.— Oh,

hear the track.— Oh, click - e - ty clack.— I'll go my mer - ry way.—

1.- 4.
E6

5.
E6

2. The — I

knew I could. I knew I could. I knew I could. I

knew I could. I knew I could. I

knew I could.

E♭6   E6

Additional Lyrics

2. The little train went rousing on so fast it seemed to fly,
   Until it reached a mountain that went almost to the sky.
   The little engine moaned and groaned and huffed and puffed away,
   But halfway to the top it just gave up and seemed to say:

   Chorus:
   I can't go on; I can't go on; I'm weary as can be.
   I can't go on; I can't go on; this job is not for me.

3. The toys got out to push but all in vain, alas, alack,
   And then a great big engine came a-whistling down the track.
   They asked if it would kindly pull them up the mountainside,
   But with a high and mighty sneer it scornfully replied:

   Chorus:
   Don't bother me, don't bother me, to pull the likes of you.
   Don't bother me, don't bother me; I've better things to do.

4. The toys all started crying 'cause that engine was so mean,
   And then there came another one, the smallest ever seen.
   And though it seemed that she could hardly pull herself along,
   She hitched on to the train, and as she pulled she sang this song:

   Chorus:
   I think I can; I think I can; I think I have a plan.
   And I can do most anything if I only think I can.

5. Then up that great big mountain with the cars all full of toys,
   And soon they reached the waiting arms of little girls and boys.
   And though that ends the story it will do you lots of good
   To take a lesson from the little engine that could.

   Chorus:
   Just think you can, just think you can, then have that understood.
   And very soon you'll start to say I always knew I could, *etc.*

The Last Hobo

Words and Music by
Tom Paxton

Moderately slow, in 2

He was born in In - ter - na -
tried his hands— at lots—
he knows ev - 'ry rail -

tion - al Falls— a long, long time a - go. He
— of jobs and— he did 'em all with pride, from
road bull— a - long the right of way, and

moved to Tu - cum - car - i when the
shoe - ing mules— and driv - in' trucks, he
ev - 'ry ho - bo jun - gle from

i - ron - work— got slow.— He was
mas - tered what— he tried.— It
New York to San - ta Fe.— He's

corn - bread___ and hard___ scrab - ble and
must have been___ Ra - mo - na; she was
looked for his___ Ra - mo - na on the

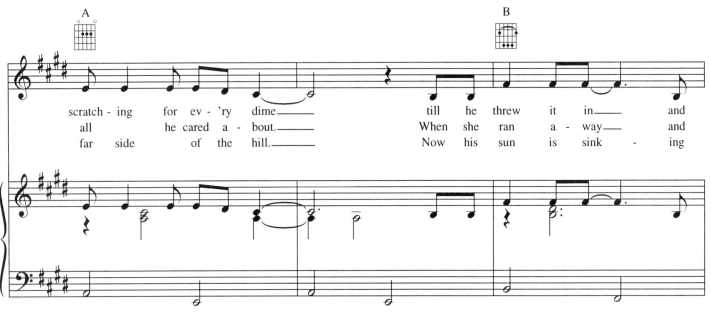

A   B

scratch - ing for ev - 'ry dime___ till he threw it in___ and
all he cared a - bout.___ When she ran a - way___ and
far side of the hill.___ Now his sun is sink - ing

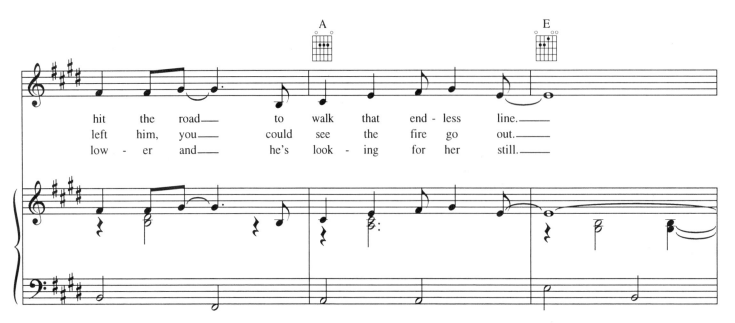

A   E

hit the road___ to walk that end - less line.___
left him, you___ could see the fire go out.___
low - er and___ he's look - ing for her still.___

57

him; once or twice____ and he would stay____ a day____ or two.____

He'd ask____ a - bout____ Ra - mo - na, then he'd say____

____ that he was on - ly pass - ing through.____

Last Train Done Gone Down

Words and Music by
Peter Rowan

61

Hoo hoo hoo_____ hoo hoo hoo hoo hoo._____

2. My sweet ba - by's on that train._____
4. I'm sor - ry for what I've done._____

My sweet ba - by's on that___ train._____
I'm sor - ry for what I've___ done._____

I won - der if I___ will see her a - gain._____
Too late,_____ good - bye,_____ my sweet ba - by cried._____

People Get Ready

Words and Music by
Curtis Mayfield

City Of New Orleans

Words and Music by
Steve Goodman

Moderately slow

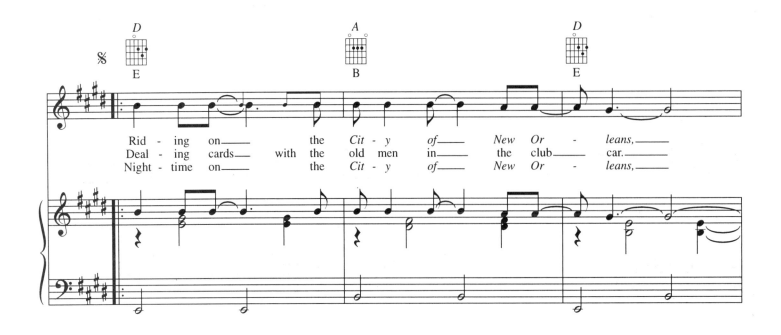

Rid - ing on_____ the Cit - y of_____ New Or - leans,_____
Deal - ing cards____ with the old men in_____ the club____ car.
Night - time on_____ the Cit - y of_____ New Or - leans,_____

three con - duc - tors and twen - ty - five sacks of mail.___
Feel the wheels___ a - rum - bling 'neath the floor.___
Mis - sis - si - pi dark - ness roll - ing down to the sea.___

All a - long a south - bound od - ys - sey,___ the
And the sons of Pull - man por - ters and___ the
But all the towns___ and peo - ple seem___ to

train pulls out of Kan - ka - kee and rolls a - long___ past
sons of en - gi - neers___ ride their fa - thers' mag - ic
fade in - to a bad___ dream, and the steel rails___

grave - yards of the rust - ed au - to - mo - biles.
rhy thm of the rails is all they feel.
This train has got the dis - ap - pear - ing rail - road blues.

Sing - ing, good morn - ing, A - mer - i - ca, how are

you? Say - ing, don't you know me,

76

Lining Track

Words and Music by
Huddie Ledbetter

Ho boys,— can't you line 'em (track— a lack)? See El - o - ise, gon - na

line 'em track. Mar - y and the babe was sit - tin' in the shade,

think - ing on the mon - ey that I— ain't made. Ho— boys,— can't you

line 'em (track— a lack)? Ho boys,— can't you line 'em (track— a lack)?

Ho boys,— can't you line 'em (track— a lack)? See El - o - ise, gon - na

line 'em track. Mos - es stood— on the Red Sea shore. Got - ta

bat - ten down the waves with a two by four.— Ho boys,— can't you

line 'em (track— a lack)? Ho boys,— can't you line 'em (track— a lack)?

Ho boys,— can't you line 'em (track— a lack)? See El - o - ise, gon - na

line 'em track. Now, if I could,— I sure-ly would————

stand on the rock where Mos-es stood. Ho———— boys,———— can't you

line 'em (track—— a lack)? Ho boys,—— can't you line 'em (track— a lack)?

Ho boys,—— can't you line 'em (track—— a lack)? See El - o-ise, gon-na

line 'em track. Mat - thew, Mark and Luke and John,— all——

—— them dis-ci - ples dead and gone. Ho———— boys,———— can't you

line 'em (track—— a lack)? Ho boys,—— can't you line 'em (track—— a lack)?

Ho boys,—— can't you line 'em (track—— a lack)? See El - o-ise, gon-na

D.S. al Coda

Coda

line 'em track. Ho—— line 'em track. *Wah!*

On CD and Audiocassette

John Denver

all aboard!

FORTIETH ANNUAL
40
GRAMMY AWARDS
WINNER
BEST MUSICAL ALBUM
FOR CHILDREN

"Both the history of our country and our musical history is in train songs. The album starts with how we settled the West, then moves into hollerin', stompin' songs, to bluegrass and to the songs the chain gangs did when they were laying down tracks. The whole idea of train songs is such a rich thing to me that I wanted to make sure it was for the whole family."

John Denver

Get the audio companion to this songbook and enjoy John Denver's tribute to trains with your entire family! CD: $13.98 and Cassette: $9.98 (suggested retail prices)

www.sonywonder.com